MW01382778

Barnyard Buddies

On the Duck Pond

by Patricia M. Stockland
illustrated by Todd Ouren

Special thanks to content consultant:
Roger Stockland, Farmer/Rancher
B.S. Agricultural Engineering, South Dakota State University

visit us at
www.abdopublishing.com

Printed in the United States.

Text by Patricia M. Stockland
Illustrations by Todd Ouren
Edited by Jill Sherman
Interior layout and design by Todd Ouren
Cover design by Todd Ouren

Library of Congress Cataloging-in-Publication Data
Stockland, Patricia M.
On the duck pond / Patricia M. Stockland ; illustrated by Todd Ouren ; content consultant , Roger Stockland.
          p.cm. – (Barnyard buddies)
Includes index.
ISBN 978-1-60270-027-7
1. Ducks—Juvenile literature. I. Ouren, Todd. II. Stockland, Roger. III. Title. IV. Series.
SF505.3.S75 2008
636.5'97—dc22

2007004685

In a coop on the farm, a mother duck rests on her nest. She is keeping her eggs warm.

Quack, quack!

A female duck is called a hen.

The hen has lined her nest with down. These small, soft feathers keep her eggs warm when she leaves her nest.

Eggs must be kept warm to hatch.

After a few weeks, the eggs start to crack.
The young ducklings break out of their shells.
They are covered in wet, yellow down.

Baby ducks are called ducklings.

After the ducklings dry off, they are ready to leave the nest. They follow their mother to the pond.

Within 24 hours of hatching, ducklings are ready to leave the nest.

The ducklings poke around the pond for insects. These juicy bugs help the ducklings grow big and strong.

Ducklings do not drink milk from their mother.

The ducklings are full. It is nap time. The brood snuggles near its mother to sleep.

A group of ducklings is called a brood.

After only four weeks, the ducklings start getting adult feathers. The young birds preen their feathers. They stretch their wings.

When ducks preen, they are cleaning
and oiling their feathers. This oil
keeps ducks waterproof.

15

After another four weeks, the ducks are fully grown. They waddle around the farm and swim in the pond.

Ducks waddle because their legs are
near the back end of their bodies.
This helps them swim.

The farmer feeds the ducks cracked corn.
When winter comes, the young ducks will
have extra weight and down to stay warm.

Farmers raise ducks for down, eggs, and meat. Ducks are also raised as pets.

Next spring, these ducks will hatch their own broods. Until then, there is plenty to do near the pond. **Quack, quack!**

Duck Diagram

bill

eye

wing

breast

foot

Glossary

brood—a group of ducklings.

coop—a small barn on a farm especially for ducks, chickens, and geese.

down—tiny feathers that keep a young bird warm.

insects—bugs.

oil—a greasy liquid that does not mix with water.

Fun Facts

A hen will protect her young while they feed. She will watch for enemies such as snapping turtles and eagles.

Female ducks have a louder quack than male ducks.

Pekin ducks are the most common type of farm duck in the United States.

Ducks have a special gland that makes the oil they spread onto their feathers. All ducks preen their feathers with this oil.

Some kinds of wild ducks will dive more than 100 feet (30 m) underwater to catch food!

A male duck is called a drake.

Hens will start quacking and clucking to their ducklings even before the ducklings have hatched.

Farm ducks cannot fly as well as wild ducks.

Index